About Michael Favala Goldman's writing:

Michael Favala Goldman is a stealth poet. The plain language and deep meaning of his poems can reverberate to the core of your being.

> – Lynette Yetter, Poetry Translation finalist 2023 PEN Awards

Goldman's poems are succinct and subtle, understated even, yet powerful and persuasive; one after another, they take the reader by quiet surprise.

> – Barry DeCarli, author of *Camouflage of Noise and Silence.*

These are the poems we need in this human moment, at the sticky end of the pandemic. Goldman's transcendent vulnerability underscores how little we have, and how precious and resilient it is, after all.

> – Sara Eddy, author of the poetry collection *Full Mouth*

What sparkles in Goldman's work is that the voice is both sweet and edgy. There is a slight tone of annoyance, a touch of anger that compliments the quiet sweetness. The clash, the juxtaposition of these forces gives way to a voice that is proper. By 'proper' I mean *real,* a series of tropes that captures the nuances of the human experience, of the human tumble down the stairs of everyday life.

> – Matthew Lippmann, author of *Mesmerizingly Sadly Beautiful,* winner of the Levis Prize in Poetry

These poems recognize the spiritual implications of quotidian moments and objects in daily life. They gently expose, with warm humor and piercing honesty, the unbridgeable separateness of each person, while also holding up for the reader examples of the sometimes difficult yet unbreakable connections between each of us.

> – Mark Luebbers, author of the poetry collection *Flat Light,* co-author of *Citizens of Ordinary Time* and the chapbook *Group Portrait.*

Michael Goldman's newest book of poetry, *Someday All of This Will Be Yours* is replete with rich narrative poems. In "The Family Game: Pinochle" he writes, "No one gloats. It is enough / to sit at the table." Goldman's poetry is like this. It is enough to sit with his images and let them flow through us.

   – Poet Lori Desrosiers' latest book is *Keeping Planes in the Air*

Pithy, poignant, thoughtful meditations on what matters most: love, aging, loss, and connection. Goldman's poems will help you see life, romance, and friendship in a more incandescent light.

   – Lanette Sweeney, author of *What I Should Have Said: A Poetry Memoir about Losing a Child to Addiction*

Goldman's poems leave us in a rich wake of stories, meanings, and contradictions inherent in being human. He transforms daily moments in fresh and playful ways, building poems everywhere, suggesting why a soul might stick around.

   – Sharon Tracey, author of *Land Marks*

Grounded and ethereal. Goldman's poems run the gamut: the pain, the pleasure, the awe, and the confusion of being. Deceptive meditations on everyday living reveal the greater truths of existence. A brilliant reminder of the magnitude experience.

   – A.M. Larks, *Kelp Journal*

Someday All of This Will Be Yours

Poems

To Susan
wik friendship
and solidarity —

Michael Favala Goldman

Cyberwit.net
HIG 45 Kaushambi Kunj, Kalindipuram
Allahabad - 211011 (U.P.) India
http://www.cyberwit.net
Tel: +(91) 9415091004
E-mail: info@cyberwit.net

Printed at VCORE LLP.

TABLE OF CONTENTS

2

3

Acknowledgments:

Felling a tree with Tommy Twilite's poetry advice

Tofu Ink Journal, summer 2021

Irony; Of course, this is just my opinion;

Weekend Project: moving furniture; David Brower

Lothlorian Journal, summer, 2021

The Prophet

Northampton Biennial, 2021

The Family Game: Pinochle; New Sexy Underwear

Meat for Tea, summer, 2021

Dance Lesson

Naugatuck River Review, 2022

The Nature of Things

The Writing is on the Walls, 2023

The ones with the split tails are terns

Kelp Review, 2023

WITH APPRECIATION TO:

Libby and Linda, and to all the people, named and unnamed, who make appearances in this book. You help me to recognize the poetry in life.

1

I'm pretty sure

the reason to read this is to get an iota closer to enlightenment
which we think is all our relationships easing
into a natural state of connection, including
the one we have with ourselves, without anxiety,
distance or boredom, and here I am thinking life
is like a bolt of fabric slowly being unrolled on the table,
a memory of patterns, the best and worst finding balance
in the material limited by its edges, and the roll unfolds
perhaps forever, never getting any better or worse:
one day we're betraying our best friends,
the next we're pleading for forgiveness,
wholeness like that, broken and mended,
never quite the same, but somehow matching
all the way down, similarly broken and mended,
which is no plea for despair or jadedness, but the opposite
more like a plea for becoming broken and mended
like the rest of our fabricked life, so we blend like camouflage –
after all it is ours. We can't escape it. I think if we do this
we will run into each other and barely be able
to distinguish where either of us begins.

Art

Each creation like a new day,
blank, and then a design all its own,
unfolding, unforeseen.

There is your offering. An extension
of what came before. It was you,
then it was yours, now it is ours.

Prophesy I

The future is now.
Always has been.

Problem is how
difficult to be now

considering the past
and the lures of fantasy.

The germ of utopia
is fertile

when the ground
of attention

meets the light
of imagination.

Irony

The ghost inside me seeks
every opportunity

to make this day
about me

each wall a mirror
each face an insult.

Or compliment.
I am here for a reason:

to pile on validation
that I'm here for a reason

and around I go
in the circle cage of days

the light changing
the leaves changing

and I wonder
where the time goes.

Words

A poor substitute
for what's happening

Whatever we say
vain arrogance

While reality remains
humbly intrusive.

The Barn Roof

It had been a discussion item for years –
the 19th century barn was choked
with cast-off furniture, boxes of records,
clothing, beds, whatever people couldn't
take with them. And the dangerous sway
of the walls wasn't worth the work
as long as the roof leaks were eroding
the timber sills and plates. Ghosts of horses
and farmers moved among the neglect.

I didn't feel like a savior, was just looking
for a way to be useful, thirty feet
above the pavement, fifty feet
above the weedy livestock yard.
I cinched a ladder to the gable peak, and with
ropes, clamps, buckets, hauled up
replacement metal panels, hand tools,
power tools, attachments points, chains,
aluminum paint, brushes, working in solitude
halfway to the sky.

Late one morning a woman from the community
walked up the driveway and shouted up to me.
The wind shuttled her words across the air.
Two planes … hit …world … center. I stood up,
faced her, toolbelt pockets resting on my thighs,
rope at my back keeping me from plunging
into gravity. I shouted back, What? She repeated,
Planes … crashed … twin … towers.

Sure I heard wrong, I waved. She waved
and tramped away. I could find out later,
whatever it was.

I was set up
with my tools and ropes
and I wasn't coming down
anytime soon. I looked up.
The sky was clear.

In my mythology

The most powerful god is Grief
who seizes things impulsively, illogically,
impervious to all except his queen,
Globus, the goddess of tears. Jimmy-Jack
is god of fun, who can stop time with just
one drop of his elixir. Mrs. Jones is the fickle
goddess of praise, presiding over schools,
contests, dividing the unworthy
from the rest, her sword so sharp and thin
it cannot be seen, only felt. Then there is Lucky,
the six-legged dog, pulling every person
through their life with his countless leashes,
which no one can let go of
nor keep up with.

Anxiety

My reality appears well-built
like scaffolding

assembled by little union
workers in my mind

sure of their jobs
and a pension.

But my view is hemmed in
by all the construction.

Don't they take
vacation?

The subtle aggression of self-improvement

You will never be good enough
but you are here
on God's good earth
to try and die trying.

You could be meditating
or volunteering
in the community
right now
instead of this.

You could be loving
someone who really needs it
or exploring
your deep dreams.

But don't just take
my word for it.

You

There you are
containing multitudes,

wondering
if anyone else notices.

Not the kind of thing that happens everyday

Jonathan bid thirty, ridiculously high
and even though I only had
five points meld and one good suit
it was the first hand
and I didn't want their team
to get the best of us right off
so I said thirty-one
and Jonathan said
are you kidding me
but then my wife
had just what I needed
for a run and we put down
thirty meld and took another twenty
in tricks which wasn't too shabby
which was when Tiina my translator
colleague sent me the message
she was reading the New York Times
book reviews tonight and
our translation was the headline:
"A sublime set of memoirs…"
and she sent me the link to the article
which I read aloud to our little foursome
with difficulty because it was through
and through a totally rave review
and I was smiling so much
while my wife filmed me. We returned
to the game and Jonathan and Renee
took the rest of the bids.

This Moment

So large.
So small.
So fitting.

Kibbutz

From the other international work/study visitors I learned you could turn the room heater horizontal to make toast or popcorn. After Hebrew class, the old teacher taught art by striking a pose and giving us ten seconds to sketch him in chalk. Later I sat in the playground making detailed pencil drawings of the sliding board: you could go up the ladder to the slide or down the steps to the bomb shelter. When Nomi caught me at the cafeteria closet spooning tahini into a jar to take back to my room, I felt ashamed, but pretended I didn't know it wasn't allowed. She made me put it back and the next day an announcement was made.

In a few words

I would like each poem
to softly disturb
interrupt and penetrate
the familiar,
create a mood
identification
with the other
or with a truth
previously ignored
now irrevocably
revealed.
Each line
a minute
discovery,
like turning over
a shell, finding
something alive
or dead,
stunning
or grotesque
something
to remember
the rest of your day
or your life,
something you want
to share and
don't want to share,
something
that elicits

a response
ties you
to the great world
and to your deep self
at the same time.

Here's what to do

When your wife loves you enough
to give up her childhood piano
which the piano tuner has condemned
which only you play everyday
and she lets you pick out the upright grand
of your choice from the twenty or so
in the dealer's church basement showroom
and you have the black Yamaha delivered,
salvage as much of the bookended
and polished mahogany from the old piano
as possible, and store it in your workshop.
Then cut squares and rectangles
from the cover, music stand, and
front panel according to a rough 1/10
scale drawing so it resembles the old piano
with the metal Jørgensen emblem
on the front and blackened mahogany
slivers for the sharps and flats.
Add two rectangles of white plastic
inscribed in black marker with favorite songs
for sheet music, glued to the tiny stand.
Shine it all with furniture polish and wrap
in tissue paper and pack in a gift box.
Give it to her and love her tears.

Dance Lesson

My grandfather
puts on Glenn Miller
and after their brief demonstration
of joyful moving
in unfathomable harmony
to the cloying rivers of sound
my grandmother escorts me
to the living room floor
leads me rhythmically
with her arms, legs, and hips,
pushing and pulling my
skinny teenage body
to join her
inside the music
perhaps so one day
I might impress
or at least not disappoint
a pretty girl who falls
for my lack of stature
and pretense.
I try to follow,
not step on her
as her knees knock
my thighs
prodding my feet
into place.

Prophesy II

You will become the you
the future has in mind

Today a consequential step
nowhere to linger

Your soul has plans
conspiring with time

And you thought you were just
sticking around.

Someday all of this will be yours

My inheritance
      is a secret.

My parents never accumulated wealth
      only a story.

The story tells why I am
      the way I am.

They tell me
      it will die with them.

They will not pass it down, though
      they already have.

They can't take away or give me
      anything precious.

Only their fear.

Whatever happened
      is still happening.

Give me
      what is rightfully mine.

All it takes

A little handful
of words.

Felling a tree with Tommy Twilite's poetry advice

for Tommy

This tree was even bigger than the one we'd brought down together.
I was going to try and drop it into a gap in the woods to the left,
but after tossing my throw bag up towards a crotch about 35 feet up –
about 20 times – I realized I had burned a hole through my glove
with the friction from the string and burned a hole through the skin
of my finger as well, so I reexamined the prospect and decided
the tree really wanted to fall to the right. The blood was minimal.

Then I stood behind this one-hundred-and-fifty foot red oak
with the twelve-foot circumference and a large black gouge
at the base where carpenter ants had chewed their way in.
I thanked the oak for the air, for the shade, for the shelter
for all the tiny creatures, for the fungi, the lichen, and now,
for the wood which will keep our house warm. I decided
to make my mouth cuts higher than usual, to guard against
any surprises from the weakened trunk.

As I leaned into the cut, I saw that the metal gripping teeth
beside the bar of the saw were missing a screw and dangling.
This was going to make the job more challenging, but I wasn't
about to stop now. I finished the first mouth cut about one-third
of the way in, just as I wanted. The second cut was more difficult,
not having leverage I would have enjoyed from the gripping teeth.
The wedge-shaped void revealed the heart of the trunk, black and punky,
even here, five feet off the ground, channeled out by the ants. But I thought
there would be enough good wood around it for my hinge.

Finally I made the back cut, easing past the center of the trunk,
about four inches above my mouth cut, until I heard a creak.
The tree tipped forward about five degrees and I stepped back
about five steps. I stepped up and cut another inch, and the tree
tipped forward a couple more degrees and stopped. I looked up.
A branch near the top on the side was leaning against a branch
of a neighboring tree. Otherwise, the oak was aimed right
in the direction I had planned. Cutting more of the hinge was risky.

So I decided to hope for wind. Then I decided to go to my shed,
grab my digging bar. Maybe I could pry into the space I had opened
with my cuts, and lever the tree past the offending branch. Considering
the tonnage of the oak, I knew it was a long shot. As I walked back
from my shed through the trees, with the iron bar on my shoulder,
there was a swishing, a crashing, several booms, breaks
and a slam, as the giant hit the earth. Call it luck, call it prayer,
call it poetry. You should have been there. It was awesome.

The moment in the virtual poetry group when I am no longer in control

A poet has shared a new poem
and another poet is responding
to the poet and to the poem,
offering a couple of suggestions
which my left brain is barely registering
because my right brain is perceiving
it all as love, pervading the 5G,
the wi-fi, the inside of my clothing, and
the hair on the back of my neck.
I am observing as the next poet offers
a couple of completely different comments
in exactly the same emotional vein,
and it's obvious we have struck it rich.
Everyone on this video call is no longer
a face in a square, or a poet seeking.
We have solved the challenges
of form and content.

Vector

Once you start moving
in a certain direction
inertia takes over.

Space is vast.
You can drift
for eternity.

There is the occasional
body with its attractive gravity
bending the course,
if you're lucky.

My crafty wife

My life is filled
with me
my opinions
my presence.

Here I am
watching
listening
talking.

And here you come
with scissors
to cut my seams.

Lovingly
you unfold the material
I didn't know
was there.

I feel small
as you iron
the wrinkles.

I hope to grow
into it.

You may have heard about this

Our bodies are atoms
in an expanse of inner space
protons, electrons, neutrons
which aren't even there all the time
as they oscillate
between matter and energy.

Underneath it all
you're naked as me
amidst all this void
barely here
the culmination of habits
and decisions.

This is us, bobbing
on the space-time ocean,
a wave continuum
breaking and breaking
on the shore of
what happens next.

2

Plunge

Getting to know you
as deep as gravity
takes longer
than I have,
hurts in a pleasant
kind of way
like a projectile
accelerating
you know
it will hit
eventually,
something
consummated,
something
destroyed.

Tantalus

It's Saturday around six am.
The light still gray.
We're naked in bed.
The usual.

I hear you sigh.
I'm careful
not to touch you
or make noise.

Don't know
your mood
or state
of wakefulness.

My body keeps wondering
a thousand awkward ways
how to approach you
this time.

So it will be different.
So you won't disappear.

Living with my subconscious

You were getting ready to leave
for your women's retreat
and I stayed out of the way
feeling slighted, because
you would rather be with them.

Later I would understand this
was both the case and not the case.
In fact, it wasn't about me, except
for how I was making it.

Feelings can be old
from long before
which I had not fathomed.

The air was charged and heavy.
I wasn't myself
not until
you closed the door
and drove away.

Heredity

Come to me, my son
when love threatens

We will toss a ball
drill holes in wood
paint a shelf

Let the women flounder.

I'd like to know you better

I'm walking down the hallway
realizing that you are not my objective
or even you,
but you are the you
I make you out to be.

And I wonder
how you have changed
while the you I know
has stayed the same.

And how you change without me
and how you can only change
if I change.

And my steps come nearer
to the bright opening
of the dining room
with the light streaming in
through the patio doors.

And there you stand,
more of you
than you.

What I Tell Myself

I am happy
you keep trying
to make me more aware of

the bed made, or unmade
the way I greet you
the nuances of the set table
a touch with a few fingers
a whole hand.

I could go on.

To live up to you
is not a destination
but a journey.

You trouble me
so completely
because you love me.

Something I've been meaning to figure out

I'm aware of my hands now
while writing
but when I'm washing my hair
I'm thinking of paperwork
waiting for me on my desk
draining my blood.

When I breathe into my back
I feel my ribs
expand like an accordion, yet
while I'm packing my groceries
I don't realize
I'm humming a song.

Then the cashier says,
"Music's nice, isn't it?"
I stop and look
at what space is left
in the bag. What will fit:
the spinach or the rolls?

When you hold me
I feel the difference
in the pressure of our arms.
I don't know
what that means.

Differences

If only I had taken a larger piece of her veggie quiche
though I don't like eggs much and she knows this
but she does like eggs, has them for breakfast
several times a week
while I have bread or cereal (sometimes I bake muffins)
and when she makes eggs for dinner, like last night
I don't say anything, I take some.
But then she said, that's not a very big piece
and I said, I'll just eat this first
and I did have seconds, though probably in total
still only half as much as she had
and when we got into a discussion later
about my inability to discern between
a conversation she feels is connecting
and one she does not, I was painted
into a corner of emotional blindness
our differences suddenly threatening
as if she were getting me back,
as if she didn't know me all along.

Relativity

You are moving away from me
faster than the speed of light

but it's not your fault
or even your velocity

it's the universe expanding
like our lives.

I see your light getting smaller
as if through a tunnel

stretching like time
though you just left

my memory's already fading
shielding me from blame

for not seeing you
when you were moving toward me.

When today's light was leaving Arcturus

I was in middle school
sitting on my girlfriend's sofa
Pink Floyd's "The Wall"
side two at a suitable
enveloping volume

both our pants unzipped
heavenly bodies turning
as they always have
in rhythmic dance

a private party
a distant star
a flash
into the void
of time and space.

What the future is for

We're sitting on the sofa.
It's past our bedtime.

There are issues between us
too long and knotty to unravel.

The part of me that wants an answer
is already sleeping, calm and deep.

Then our eyes meet in a way that says,
"I choose you. And I will keep choosing you."

Bernoulli, you, and me

Making my way
around you
is not the same
as with other people.

It's not just your shape
(though, that too).

There's farther to go
negative pressure
a lift
and my symmetry is gone.

Beloved

You receive the light
from my fire
and disperse it
among the stars.

New Sexy Underwear

You can't see it –
the almost smile.

The Tao says
keep your jewels hidden.

All day a private knowing,
delight in nearly nothing.

There is a lot going on

The light outside.
My heart beating.

Electrons dancing
alone and together.

Who knows
where this is heading.

Convergence

As we were watching the rioters
swarm the Capitol, break windows,
and storm down the hallways, an alarm went off
in our house. I checked the kitchen appliances,
the smoke detectors, the computers, finally ending up
in the basement, looking at a little white box on the ceiling
with a red light flashing and beeping. I opened windows, turned
on a fan, checked Google and called the fire department.
They told us to evacuate. Carbon monoxide is poisonous,
invisible and odorless.

So the three of us bundled up, shot
baskets in the driveway in sub-freezing temperatures
until the fire crew arrived in helmets, masks, boots, gloves,
marched into the house, tested the air, the gas appliances,
and proclaimed it safe to return.

We decided it had to be the wood stove not getting enough air
when the damper was closed. We thanked them; they marched out.
Then our son laid into the two of us for not wearing COVID
masks while we were outside. He said he was fed up
and he was leaving as soon as possible. We were so
irresponsible. We wanted to talk it through, but he
flat out refused.

Congress returned and counted the electoral votes.
We resolved to clean out the wood stove,
after it cooled down.

Stamina

Whatever is wrong
stays wrong
as long as
you can stand it.

The family game: Pinochle

My grandmother and I sit adjacent
at the dining room table.

I am just old enough to learn
about suits and tricks.

By small dishes of pretzels, apple slices,
nuts and raisins we play open-handed.

I have a cheat sheet for how to score
meld and how much to bid.

Four aces or a run give the most, but
I like the marriage of hearts.

The ace of spades is obviously in charge.
The jack of diamonds and queen of spades

are paramours worth four. My grandfather
a large, gentle man, who never smokes or curses,

sits across from me,
putting his cards in order.

No one gloats. It is enough
to sit at the table.

Weekend Project: moving furniture

It was your idea
to reconfigure rooms.

I follow along
trying not to upset you.

You get sad
then angry

because I'm not
taking ownership.

You expected us
to do this together.

We stop working
and talk.

Now you're crying.
I wasn't aware

there was a problem.
I failed you, again.

The one room
is looking quite good.

The hallway clogged
with things

that don't have
an obvious destination.

Two Paths

I lead us to the left
a fifty percent chance
of ending up
on a logging trail
to nowhere

just brush
mountain laurel
uneven footing
as you speak of aging
diminishing strength
while I'm concentrating
on the position
of the sun

and your knees
have had enough
we're bushwhacking
up and down ridges
you're hobbling
like Frankenstein

I'm trying to lead
you back the easiest way
to somewhere safe
away from me.

Becoming comfortable with discomfort

You think you didn't ask for this.
Whatever you're going through
is a response to chances you missed
when you could have opened
to your breaking point, instead
of adding another layer. Karma
has all the patience in the world,
keen edges that know
just where your tender spots are.
Parrying discomfort is just a way
of asking it to come around
again, and again, and again.

Things you forgot to do

Talk to your mother.
Drink more water.
Vacuum under the bed.
Defrost the food.
Write back about the agenda.
Put the check in the mail.
Use less salt.
Call about the ceiling.
Resolve your childhood fear.
Buy that gift.
Stop the bullshit.

Learning to follow

You traveled to Maine to visit a friend,
take care of her four-year-old son
as a big favor, and I came too.

You took him to the beach, fed him,
played games, gave baths,
suffered his tantrums and found
the glass chess pieces he had hidden
in a metal box along with some popcorn.

Meanwhile I tied his shoes, read stories,
built a sandcastle, a practice run
for becoming a grandfather.

I could have stayed home and
done things that were waiting.
You smiled more than I did.
Like vitamins, I didn't like the taste,
but I think it was good for me.

Controlled Hallucinations

I can't know everything about you
without knowing every electron
in every star and every drop
of blood in every damp frog.

The computer in my brain
is wild as a black hole
leaving a milk mustache
of photons on my lips.

I'm not sure I want to take you in
all the way, because I would have to
come along too, and the ten thousand things
frighten me no end.

So have mercy. Let me perceive you
slowly to the edge of the universe
and we will drop in together
when neither of us is watching.

Winter Solstice I

You're standing in the driveway
low light everywhere

except for the brightness
of your face

as if you were entangled
with a star

I'm looking at you
thinking happiness

wondering
did I bring this on

Is this ever what you see
looking at me?

Spring returning

the old songs
brighter mornings

warmer days
milder evenings

forgetting is easy
but the heart remembers

you came back

I didn't know
I could come back too.

The Core

I lean back
against your chest
feel the earth
turning
with us
as its axis.

3

On this, the coldest day

I was thinking that the yellow painted butterflies
could lift off this glass
flutter around the room
to my delight
and theirs

but they're trapped
barely alive
barely twitching
atoms and molecules
the only movements
so slight
faintly reminiscent of freedom.

I don't know if they will ever
break out,
or break out
before they break.

The Prophet

There is a humble plant growing
on forest floors in my region. Maybe
it's a fern or a stunted shrub. I have not
been able to identify it;
not yet anyway.

When you had a panic attack (I hope
you don't mind my mentioning this)
and we went for a walk to help you
calm down, we crouched and caressed
this plant's tiny cedar-like fronds.

I asked you, Do you think this plant knows
something about climate change? (I always
treat anxiety with science). Where does it
fall on the issue? Is it migrating indifferently
or desperately across the landscape?

This little being could be trying to tell us
how to meet this crisis, something
which sums it all up into one perfect
inclusive statement, and what good is it
if we are unable to listen.

I think I know how you feel

You were the one
who attracted attention
or the one who behaved
or the one who sat
at the table leg.

Beneath needing to belong
is this aloneness
which won't go away
not ever.

We're not meant
to be solitary,
so what is aloneness
doing there, driving us
into the arms of others
then pushing them away
while the aloneness alone
remains hard and unchanged.

I get the feeling
nature never feels alone.

Join your aloneness
to mine.

I think we were meant
to be together.

Welcome to the family

Rootstock
An incision

A foreign scion
A ring

All future fruit
will spring from this.

Short Memory

We say Happy New Year
even though life is suffering.
Well, maybe not completely,
but each rolling wave
buries the previous one.
If any of them are happy
what difference does it make.
Words pale before deeds and events.
Not that I have anything against hope
or good wishes, but after midnight
we will revert to what we know.

The nature of things

He stretches his long blue neck
then pulls it back as regally
as possible with the red snood
hanging down. She stands
six feet away. He raises his fan
of brown tail feathers, revealing
white shafts and speckled pillow
of finer feathers below and pale
patterned down below that,
and she is not even looking
as he turns 360 degrees,
the sun catching bronze
between his wings as hesitantly
he lowers his treasures and steps
in synch with his mate
still distant over to the leaf pile
where they scratch
each to their own, peck
at what might be there.
He raises his tail again,
this time only halfway.

Octopus

She's not coming out
not while you're there.

She's too soft
a body.

She has all the time in the world
and would sooner starve.

You can't pull her out
she'd rather lose a limb.

You can wait.
Willingness and patience

on the surface of your skin.
Forget what you've gained or lost.

It's not about you.

Job Creator

He shakes my hand
warmly and jovially
while his largesse
is slowly undermining
the foundation of life.

Capitalist

I was never initiated
into the fine gymnastics
of putting oneself
into another's shoes which
I don't know about you but
for me is harder than it sounds.

So forgive me for giving the wrong
impression by creating a decaying
world view of skyscrapers, glass
displays and floating hygiene garbage.
Try putting yourself in my place.
Think how I must feel.

Common Denominator

Electro-magnetic radiation is so stable
we receive pictures from Mars
like letters in the mailbox.

Someone is inventing, or has,
a telescope to look through and see
the effect of the Big Bang.

Meanwhile 18% of Worcester
residents are not alone
in having no internet.

How is virtual learning
working for your family?
Have you learned to dance?

There's no proof the future exists

It's easy to blame the past
harder to stop it perpetuating.

The future seems like
it could be easier

but only because
it never happened.

Vacation

I have cancelled
the newspaper
and the mail.

Disconnected
as life was
decades ago.

There's a hollow
in my volition
waiting for intuition.

Maybe
I won't
get up today.

Sunday Cleaning

My piano was made in Japan
though the components
probably were sourced more widely.

The dust settled on the black finish
is less easy to place.

I read that dust from Vesuvius
is still in the air. And what about the dust
from my grandmother's antiques?

Even if you could identify
each particle
(under magnification)
are time and place
even worth mentioning?

Wiping it clean
is blasphemous
and sacred.

Fall Equinox

Now is the time
to spread seeds
on the bare spots.
around the equinox
all nature accelerates,
even you, as you strew
the tiny grains,
people are starting school,
changing jobs,
holding craft fairs,
perhaps out of knowledge
of winter,
an ancient impulse that wonders
will we make it through.
We broadcast seeds
with a 77% chance
something will come up.

Boulder Field

Lake Harmony, Pennsylvania

If I could compress
20,000 years into one moment
it would be elemental
bedrock shattering
eroding, shifting,
roiling
and then
silence.

Barely a bird
crossing the barrenness,
a failed tree,
pieces that do not quite fit,
poor footing,
my presence
or absence
inconsequential.

Of course, this is just my opinion

It could go one way or the other.
Either the spring builds up, trickles
or geysers at the surface, or stays
a blind current buried. Yes or no used to be
without explanation, a reaction
to readiness. Then the stairway of logic
built higher and higher in response
to the questioning, as the floor dropped
stepwise farther into the basement.
It's all a construction.

River

Who can slip a stone from a mountain.
bear it to the shore, all the while
tumbling, tumbling smooth, until
it is hardly recognizable, yet still
that stone, now nearly glowing
with an inner light. Who can do this
with numberless stones, yet never become
bored, tired or careless.

David Brower

Glen Canyon, 1956

The river was still undammed,
cliffs visible,
wildlife unknowing
their fate.

When the water rose
some would proliferate,
some disappear,
and people would come
on jetskis and in rental
canoes, not as well-equipped
as this canoe parked
on the bank.

Though the executive order
had been set in motion
the river was still free,
and he didn't know,
he could still see
nature according to itself
as he sat on a log,
his grilled steak sagging
slightly over the edges
of his Sierra Club cup.

That night under the stars
he dreamed of living
under the water
with all the happy creatures.

Cold Comfort

Let the snow come
cover the truth.

I don't want
to see it anymore.

Prayer

Not what you say,
not what you think.
In silence
what you hear.

Not what you think,
not what you've been told.
What you hear
when all else is gone.

Not what you've been told,
not what everyone else is doing.
When all else is gone
this is what begins.

Not what everyone else is doing,
not what you say.
This is what begins
in silence.

Leaf Gathering

Have you noticed it has been
a banner year for leaves
and a bad year for patience?

Usually neither require
more than cursory attention.
Their natural rise and wane.

But this year leaves and patience
are on opposite trajectories.

And I am out in my yard
trying to collect them both.

Habituated

I no longer think
there is anything strange

about leaving the house
close to midnight

to walk in a field
in the freezing cold

so the blue moon
can brighten our faces

give us night shadows
light our path

though usually
there is no reason

to do anything
of the kind.

The ones with the split tails are terns

And if you watch them fly into the wind
you will lose your balance and fall
onto the soft sand.

And don't be tempted to pull up the dune grass
it is the only thing
keeping the continent in place.

The wind and moon work in concert –
the Creator, if you will,
while you are a very recent visitor,

a tourist with slow-growing roots
causing accidental damage
every day.

To become part of nature
you must observe closely
and remain in one place.

The Difference

I'm walking through the cemetery.
I lift my hands to the sky and say,
"Rejoice!"
Not a spirit stirs.
(Except mine.)

Stop in time

The best of life
cooks down
to one paradoxical
essence.

If you have to
think about it
you've already gone
too far.

Winter Solstice II

This is as far as we go
into the cold and dark
dotted with stars

turning, turning back
into the pull
that feels like home

we move and remain
nearly timeless
nearly unperturbed

old forces hold sway
shrug off inertia
keep us going

where light
makes everything
possible.

WORKS BY MICHAEL FAVALA GOLDMAN

POETRY:
Who has time for this?
Small Sovereign
Slow Phoenix
If you were here you would feel at home
This May Sound Familiar
Someday all of this will be yours
What Minimal Joy

TRANSLATIONS:
Poetry:
Farming Dreams – Selected Poems of Knud Sørensen
Average Neuroses – Selected Poems of Marianne Koluda Hansen
Inheritance – Selected Poems of Cecil Bødker (2018)
Something to Live Up To – Selected Poems of Benny Andersen vol. 1
Certain Days – Selected Poems of Benny Andersen vol. 2
Selected Poems – Erik Knudsen
New and Selected Poems – Knud Sørensen

Prose:
Fragments of a Mirror – Selected Essays of Knud Sønderby
Stories about Tacit – Cecil Bødker
The Water Farm – Cecil Bødker
Malvina – Cecil Bødker
The Way It Seems – Selected Short Stories of Knud Sørensen
Liberated – Selected Essays of Suzanne Brøgger
The Starveling – Cecil Bødker
Dependency – Tove Ditlevsen
The Trouble with Happiness – Selected Short Stories of Tove Ditlevsen

CHILDREN'S BOOKS:

From Out of the Blue – Rebecca Bach-Lauritsen and Anna Margrethe Kjærgaard